STN

THIS WALKER BOOK BELONGS TO:

_ _ _ _ _ _ _ _ _ _ _ _ _ _ _ _

_ _ _ _ _ _ _ _ _ _ _ _ _ _ _ _

_ _ _ _ _ _ _ _ _ _ _ _ _ _ _ _

First published 2020 by Walker Books Ltd
87 Vauxhall Walk, London SE11 5HJ

This edition published 2021

10 9 8 7 6 5 4 3 2 1

Text © 2020 Sally Sutton
Illustrations © 2020 Brian Lovelock

The right of Sally Sutton and Brian Lovelock to be identified as the author and illustrator respectively of this work has been asserted by them in accordance with the Copyright, Designs and Patents Act 1988

This book has been typeset in Anton and Block T

Printed in China

British Library Cataloguing in Publication Data:
a catalogue record for this book is available from the British Library

ISBN 978-1-5295-0337-1

www.walker.co.uk

WHEELS

SALLY SUTTON • ILLUSTRATED BY BRIAN LOVELOCK

WALKER BOOKS

AND SUBSIDIARIES

LONDON • BOSTON • SYDNEY • AUCKLAND

**Rumbly wheels, grumbly wheels,
Hauling-up-the-hill wheels.**

*Wheels go fast, wheels go slow.
Shout what's coming, if you know!*

Lorry! Lorry!

Watch it go!

Whizzy wheels, busy wheels,
Roaring-up-the-road wheels.

**Wheels go fast, wheels go slow.
Shout what's coming, if you know!**

Motorbike! Motorbike!

Watch it go!

Snazzy wheels, jazzy wheels,
Picking-people-up wheels.

**Wheels go fast, wheels go slow.
Shout what's coming, if you know!**

Taxi! Taxi!

Watch it go!

**Zoomy wheels, vroomy wheels,
Racing-to-a-fire wheels.**

Wheels go fast, wheels go slow.
Shout what's coming, if you know!

Fire Engine! Fire Engine!

Watch it go!

**Yucky wheels, mucky wheels,
Carting-off-the-waste wheels.**

**Wheels go fast, wheels go slow.
Shout what's coming, if you know!**

Rubbish truck! Rubbish truck!

Watch it go!

**Bumpy wheels, dumpy wheels,
Bouncing-round-the-town wheels.**

Wheels go fast, wheels go slow.
Shout what's coming, if you know!

School bus!
School bus!

Watch it go!

Tiny wheels, shiny wheels,
Having-heaps-of-fun wheels.

Wheels go fast, wheels go slow.
Shout what's coming, if you know!

Scooter! Scooter!

Watch us go!

PARTS OF A WHEEL

Rim: The outer edge of the wheel, made of strong metal.

Hub: The middle part of the wheel, which keeps it spinning and attached to the vehicle.

Tyre: The wheel's outer covering, made of rubber and filled with air.

Tread: The outer surface of the tyre that touches the road. It has grooves and notches.

Valve: You can pump up the tyre through the valve.

Locking wheel nuts: Hold the wheel on the vehicle.